Praise For Dean Fraser

MEDIA

Here is travel writing with a difference… one poet travelling with a quest to know more; and carrying a notebook and pen!

"Dean Fraser sees his mission in life to spread some much-needed laughter and love in this world" INDIE SHAMAN MAGAZINE

AUDIENCE MEMBERS FROM HIS LIVE SHOWS

"Listening to Dean Fraser transports you. Powerful works"

"Really enjoyed listening. I loved it, well done"

"Dean was very interactive with the audience afterwards and from that, he has offered to come back to do a session on how to meditate – a request from the audience"

2021 published by Alive to Thrive Ltd

Copyright © Dean Fraser 2021

Dean Fraser has asserted his right under the Copyright, Designs and Patents Act 1988 to be identified as the author of this book and work.

All rights reserved. No part of this publication may be reproduced, stored in a retrieval system or transmitted in any form or by any means, electronic, photocopying, recording or otherwise, without the prior permission of the copyright owner.

ISBN 9798453726110

The Kent Poems

Celebrating The Garden of England!

Dean Fraser

This book is dedicated to the memory of MCC; she proved the best guide to showing me the uniqueness of Kent that I could have ever wished for.

Contents

	Page Number
INTRODUCTION	07
BENCH LOOKING OUT TO SEA ON THE KENT COAST	09
MY MARTELLO	12
DOVER TO DEAL AND BACK AGAIN	13
SANDWICH AND NO NAME AT LUNCHTIME	17
FARADAY SAID SO (DUNGENESS)	19
HOP PICKING AND LOVE	21
MARGATE LOOKING FOR TURNER	23
MARLOWE	24
PANTILES, TUNBRIDGE WELLS	25
DOVER TO CALAIS 2005	27
CHATHAM MARINA	29
THE RIVER MEDWAY	30
RECULVER TOWERS HERNE BAY	32
I LOVE FOLKESTONE	34
PORT OF SHEPPEY	36
TONY	37
PROMENADING IN HYTHE	38
GRAVESEND PIER	40

NOT SO BLEAK HOUSE, BROADSTAIRS	41
RETURNING TO ROCHESTER	43
DREAMS OF KENT	45
TRYING TO AVOID THOMAS BECKET	47
THERE WAS NO POSSIBILITY OF TAKING A WALK THAT DAY	48
HAPPY DAYS AT BRIDGE	49
FINDING VAN GOGH IN RAMSGATE	51
DARTFORD ON THE MAP	52
CHATHAM NAVAL MEMORIAL	53
TONBRIDGE TIMES	54
THE MAN WHO CHANGED EVERYTHING	55
IT MUST BE FALDO	57
FAVERSHAM MARKET	58
TALISMAN FOR SITTINGBOURNE	59
SHE WAS A TEACHER	60
THE COLDRUM STONES	61
VISITING FOLKESTONE IN WINTER	62
THE LONGER JOURNEY	63

Introduction

These tales have been inspired and written about places I have visited over the years in the beautiful Garden of England and the people I encountered along the way. Some of these are those I met, others from the past brought to life once again through the power of words.

I have spent a lot of time in Kent, coming to love and appreciate the county through travelling extensively across the whole area.

I always see my poetic tales as windows offering glimpses into a frozen moment of time, rather like seeds trapped in amber and this collection takes snapshots from the moments when I visited the locations in question.

Thank you kindly for purchasing my book. Enjoy this collection as much as I enjoyed writing it for you.

Dean Fraser

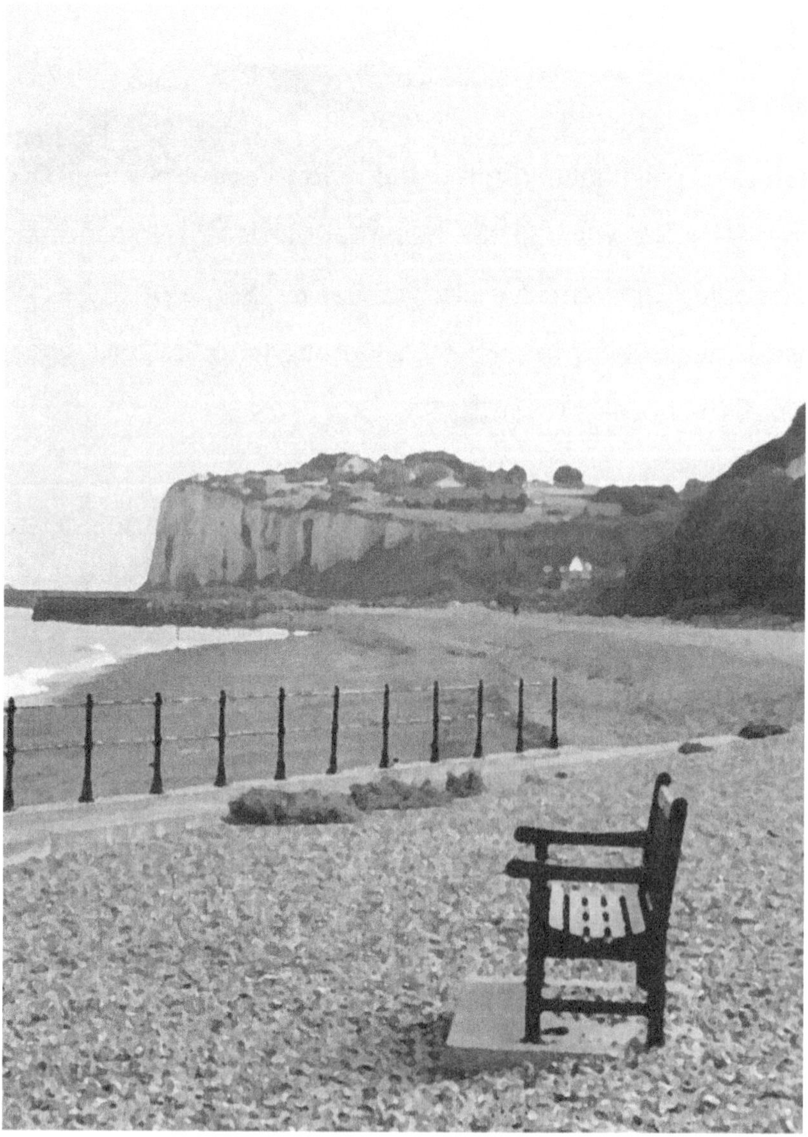

Bench Looking Out To Sea On The Kent Coast

The bench in question is situated at St Margaret's Bay, between Dover and Deal.

I am here before dawn
A halo of light appears on the horizon
As the sun slowly rises
Nature's morning light show plays out before me
Crimson, purple and yellow hypnotically colour the sky
Making way for the azure blue of this summer's day

Daylight reveals highways of the sea shimmering in the heat haze
Dover to Calais ferries dart between the wake of mammoth container ships
Walkers begin to processional pass by on their way to The Cliffs
Few pay me attention

An elderly woman with a walking stick stops
She leans on the convenient railings near me

Bidding me "good morning"
I agree that it is indeed an extremely good morning
She seems pleased with my confirmation of her certainty
As she smiles, slowly making her way back to her nearby home

Tranquillity on this bench
A man on a mountain bike rides past
Surprised to recognise the rider as someone I know
Today he fails to stop and pass some time with me
Too intent on his exercise

I eat my lunch
Prepared in advance
Prepared whilst most of the world still slept
Observing once more the ferries
I too have travelled their route
Today my role is observation
All life going on
I look upwards towards The Cliffs
Snakes of people walk the well-trodden paths
I have also walked their route
Today is altogether more leisurely

It is calm

The glistening sea

I have witnessed it untamed.

Nature unleashed

Today gentle waves lap to shore on the little beach

Here children play

Their shouts of excitement take me back to my own childhood

Different beach

Another coast

The same feeling pervades, nonetheless

Early evening the need for more sustenance calls me

Taking my leave from the bench for a little while

A solitary seagull takes my place as sentinel

In my absence he observes

I return within the hour

The seagull sentinel is gone

He must have found other adventures more enticing

Or perhaps the need for sustenance took him away as well

I take over his post

There on our bench

My watch now

A kayak passes by protectively close to shore
The bright red of a lifejacket keeps him safe
As he resolutely paddles against the tide.
To disappear out of sight around the headland
Heading for Dover I suppose
Or maybe Folkestone

The sun begins to set behind me
As darkness slowly rises across the water
Then sudden silence
Reaching outwards with all my senses
I see the lights of unknown ships
Mirrored by lights from distant silhouetted homes above me

One bench looking out to sea on the Kent Coast
Time-shared with a seagull
There is magic in the air this day
In this seascape
For those remaining still long enough to feel it

My Martello

Since the first time I became aware of Martello Towers I have had a dream to turn one into a home. No3 at Folkestone, Kent would do very nicely…

Incredible views standing looking out to sea
Always thought what a great home it could be
No1 and 2 both residentially converted long ago
No3 invitingly waiting for me to give it a go

Round Buildings work for me in an appealing way
Windmills, lighthouses, and it will happen someday
A Martello Tower in Folkestone all of my own
Who could possibly want any other kind of home?

Dover To Deal And Back Again

Inspired by one of the most spectacular of walks.

Kent's most famous feature our destination

This time to be explored on foot

A walk down through history

Well perhaps a little

Arriving via the strange looping road

Dover is busy today

Car park crowded out

Needing only one space we wait

Patience pays off once more

We are here for adventure

Today the role is interactive

Back-pack heavy with provisions to sustain

It is warm this summer's day

Dover Castle is passed on by this time

Seagulls sound pleased to see us

Setting out to see what we encounter

Steep footpath leads upwards to the cliffs

Those famous White Cliffs

Eleven miles this walk, so they say

First vantage point reached

Crystal clear tannoy announcements from port below

Poised ready on to walk onwards

This way trod by millions before us

Enjoying this elevated treat for the senses

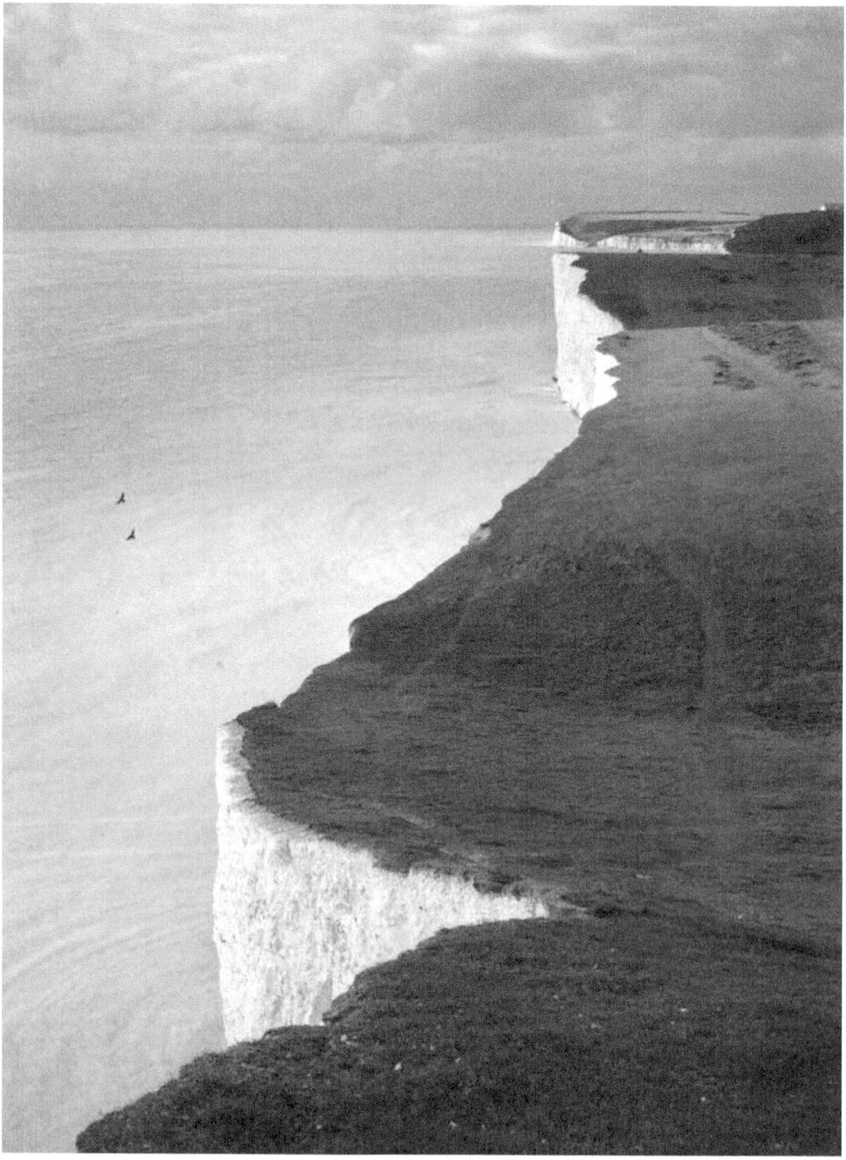

Entranced with the view

Safely still looking where we tread though!

Enchanted and delighted with the butterflies

flitting from flower to bush all around us

Eventually descending

Past stunning homes

With even more stunning views

St Margaret's Bay and a rest is in order

Taking on bottled water and raisins

Standing a while observing

Watching sunlight reflected in the water

Tearing ourselves away eventually

Onwards to see what the deal is with Deal

Walking the shaley beach

Shouts of happiness from small children

Playing down by the seashore

Deal Castle intrigues in design

Stood there to attention in the mid-day sun

Boats line the beach

We make a beeline for the pier

Apparent home to fishing folks of all ages

Mixed feelings upon arrival
Being plant-base and fish-free ourselves
Finding a convenient bench with sea view
Lunch enjoyed and suitably rested, what next?

Best laid plans are ignored
Intention had been to walk one way
The bus with which to return
A decision now viewed to derision
As back towards Dover we walk
Retracing steps for a new experience
And it is different for sure
Paths quieter for the return journey

Back on the cliffs we take our time
Savouring the views
Savouring the beauty all around us
Twenty-two miles we walked that day
Bonhomie and happiness made large
Exploration over, taking our leave of Dover
For now…

Sandwich And No Name At Lunchtime

Finding myself in Sandwich at lunchtime, I determined I would avoid the cliché of eating a bready treat of a meal...

In Sandwich wandering and wondering
Looking all around at the scenery peering
No Name Street as always puts a smile on my face
Pondering again how they chose to name the place

Seems from where I stood and observed
Sandwich is apparently more than served
Eating opportunities covering more square feet

Than every other shop in the town, on every street

Pondering as I walk, what to eat today?
Pub lunch, fine dining or quaint café?
I gorgeous sandwich shop I espied
I said I wouldn't buy one, I lied!

Faraday Said So (Dungeness)

Michael Faraday decreed the lighthouse was to be the first to have permanent electric power…

Lighthouses seemingly come and go here
Eight in all over the years
Weather and the changing landscape heeding change

Wyatt's tower buildings still stands
I wonder how much it might cost to purchase
If it were for sale; for I do so like round houses

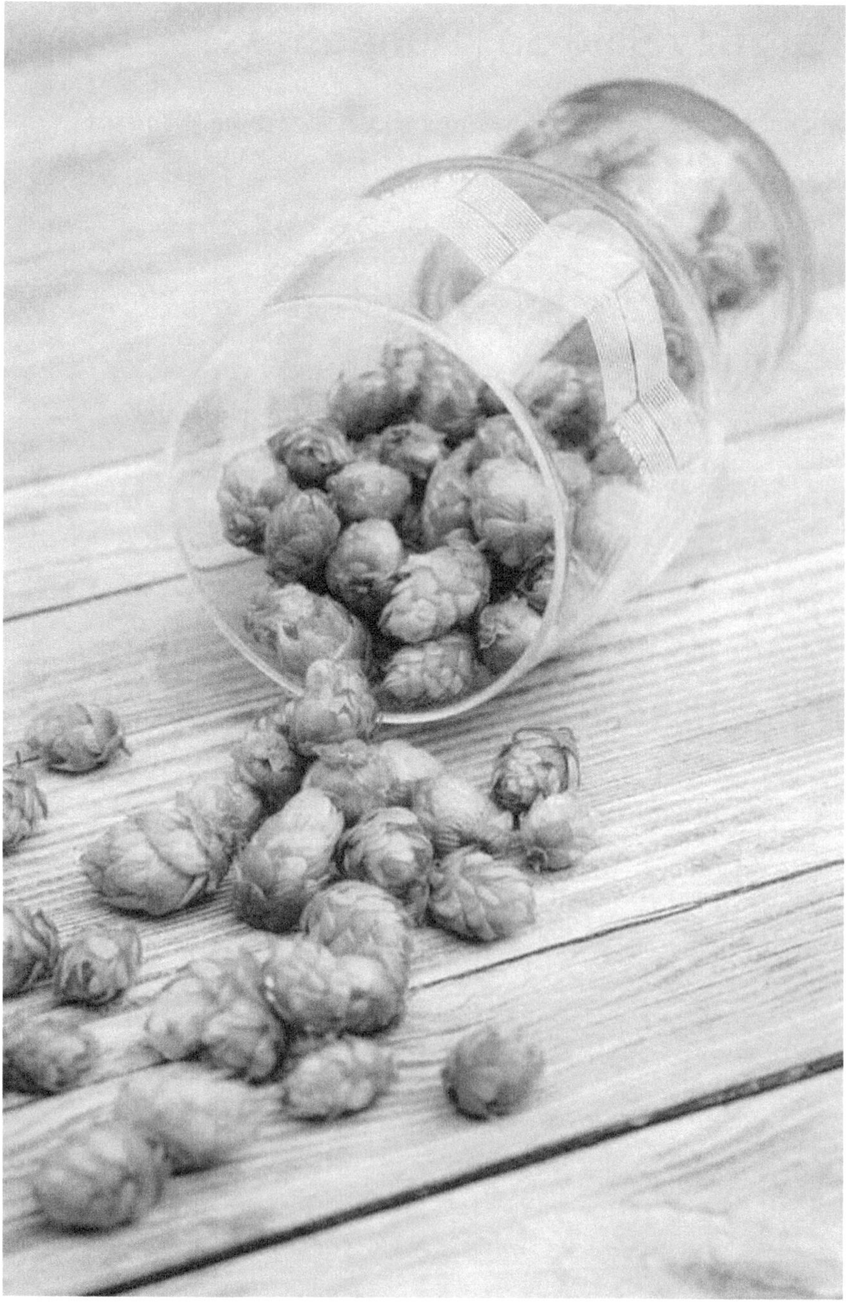

Hop Picking And Love

A story I felt compelled to share and it does bring a lump to my throat whenever I perform this poem...

Desperate poverty in The East End of London all too true
Ten-year-old Alice never complained, what good would it do?
She had reached the age to travel with her family to Kent.
Leaving behind the dirt and smog, their struggle to pay rent

Hop picking in 1920 the children did their share of grafting
Alice loved the clean air, the food, the banter and chatting
She fell in love with Kent; she dared to dream of another life
Far away from her London with all its grimness and strife

Every and every year Alice looked forward as harvest came
She was twenty now, as she travelled the train once again
Alone this time, her family had work to keep them at home
Alice saw the familiar fields, familiar friends she never felt alone

This year her long held dream of Kentish life came true
In the village she met William, they walked out those two
Getting to know one another better, bashfully a little flirty

They fell in love through the long, hot summer of 1930

Local man William asked Alice if they could wed
Barely able speak, in shock she nodded her head
Kentish life she adored with all her heart and soul
At long last Alice felt in love, complete and whole

Three generations later here in the twenty first century
Their great grandchildren continue with the family legacy
Hops, beer and a micro-brewery, the tradition unbowed
If Alice and William look down upon them, they must feel duly proud

Margate Looking For Turner

A poem paying homage to the painter J.M.W Turner, famous for his incredible skies and amongst other views, the vistas he painted of Margate where he lived at that time.

Our pilgrimage in honour of his art
To nourish the soul, culture impart
Margate on this Autumn day to contemplate
Mentally travelling back in time to appreciate

Centuries on would he recognise the views?
Were he to stand here now, wearing our shoes
Genius of a bygone age, his legacy lives right on
A prize named after him, this creative paragon

Wandering and wondering continued our arty quest
Margate overlooking the sea, we linger a moment to rest
And it happens, we look at one another, as happy tears we cry
Laid out before us, the view he saw, and above a Turner sky

Marlowe

St George's Street, Canterbury
Blue plaque sits upon the wall
Christopher Marlowe, Dramatist
Baptised in this Church 26th February 1564
So it proclaims

And Canterbury is where his story began
Going on to make his mark on the World
Still known and revered to this day
A theatre named after him in his home city

Playwright, poet, all-round creative genius.
Was he a spy? Did he influence Shakespeare?
We will probably never know for sure
Just as we will never know for sure how he died

I feel sure he would have enjoyed the mystery…

Pantiles, Tunbridge Wells

This beautiful open area at the heart of the town gets to tell its own story…

So many changes
And still I remain
Wells discovered in the 17th Century
Made me the place to visit
Queen Mary's Wells back then
My Royal connection assured
Upper and Lower Walks

So many changes
And still I remain
Pantiles are lain giving me my name
Colonnades built to enhance my beauty
The public free to wander around me
I would remain an open space from now on
Appreciated by so many

So many changes
And still I remain

Jazz is heard all around me

Bands play in my bandstand for all to enjoy

Culture for the people of now Tunbridge Wells

A market bringing those from far and wide

In homage to my uniqueness

So many changes

And still I remain

The landscape has changed around me

Down through the centuries

Some things will never change though

I am the eyes of the Royal Town

I am The Pantiles

Dover To Calais 2005

SeaCats provided a quick way to cross The Channel back in those days, being a foot passenger had never been such good value at under £20 each!

Sleek boat awaits our boarding

Gleaming white catamaran

Excitement

This is a day trip for us

Watching the normal ferry leaving Dover

Knowing we would be in Calais sooner than they

Out on deck this warm July day in 2005

As we are underway

Wash streaming out behind us

Feeling the wind in our hair

As we race across The Channel

Leaving behind The White Cliffs

Soon docking at Calais

Strolling forth to the railway station

For a day of exploring Boulogne-Sur-Mer

Arriving back early in Calais

Budget buys at warehouses holding little interest

We relax on the beach to wait…

2005 Dover to Calais and back

We weren't to know it at the time

Our mode of transport soon consigned to history

Perhaps the tunnel rendered it obsolete?

Seems such a shame really

At least we got to enjoy those magical times

Chatham Marina

A tale of distraction...

Poetry events now my motivation for visiting
Quoting prose or rhymes I've been scribbling
Back in the day took my partner to visit the town
She got quite bored, looking at me with a frown
The Marina is the reason, it caught my attention
Beautiful yachts well worth a mention
Standing in the rain, admiring the construction

Falling in raptures… genius my considered deduction
My partner not really exactly sharing my glee
Getting soaking wet and looking daggers at me
"Can we go get a coffee?" She dragged me away
From the beautiful boats that had led me astray

The River Medway

From time to time The River Medway likes to remind people it is there...

Full moon reflected in its mirror like surface

The sun creating crystal sparkles

As they are dancing magically all around

Ancient watercourse way

Originating in the hills of Sussex

Passing through Tonbridge, Maidstone and Medway

Finding The Thames Estuary at Sheerness

Dividing Kent into two parts

Once vital for powering mills along its banks

A story now told through fading photographs

Fading group memory

A place of unseen mysteries

And hidden danger within the serene waterscape

Sometimes flooding homes and businesses

Reminding us humans we are after all quite small compared to nature

Photo by Scott Chambers on Unsplash

Reculver Towers Herne Bay

The iconic twin towers dominate the landscape...

Reculver Towers are a ruin now

Once a Roman Fort stood atop its hill

Then a monastery in its place

Finally a church nearly a millennia ago

Our past facsimiled into stone

The lives of our ancestors

Walking and feeling the past

It's still alive here

For those staying quiet long enough to know

Peaceful inspiration enjoyed

And it seems the shade of the towers is perfect for us this hot day

The grass is made for our purpose

With our backs to the tower

The perfect place for yoga

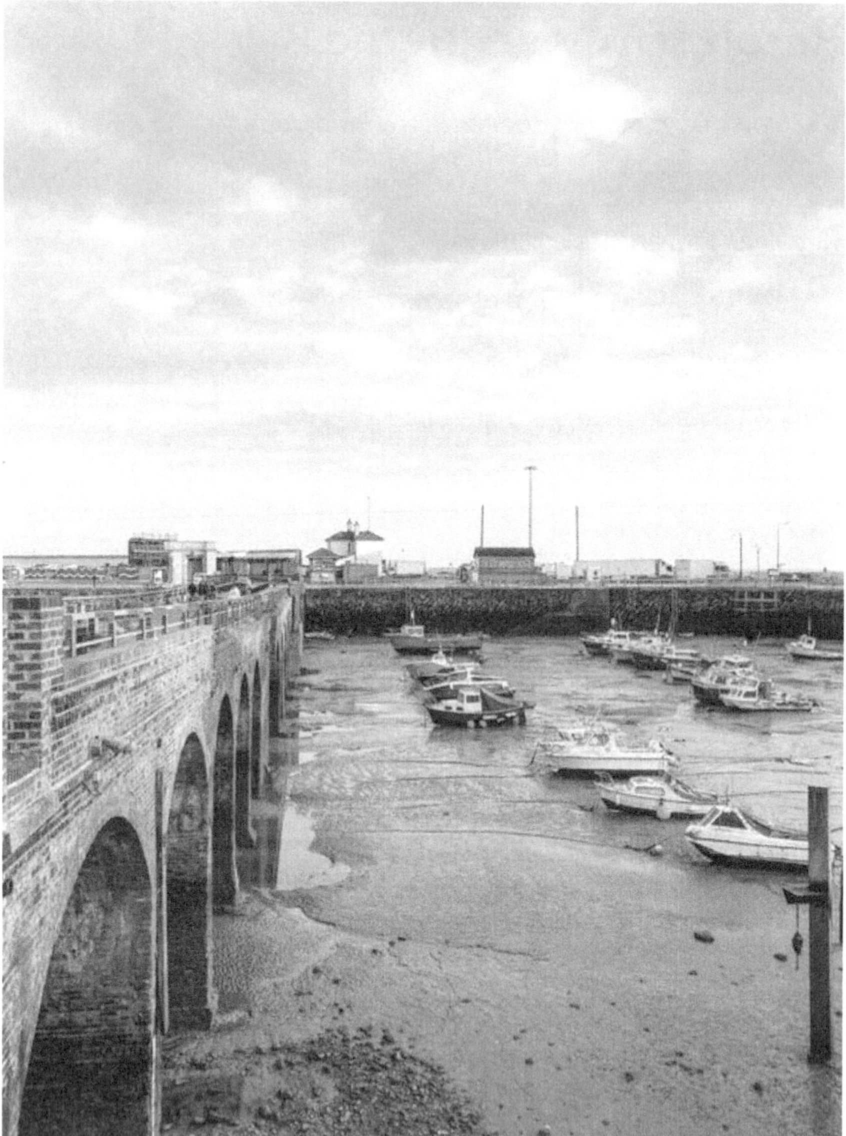

I Love Folkestone

I guess everyone will have their own favourite area or town in Kent... this is mine

We adore Folkestone, Kent
Spend time there whenever we can
Sense of belonging
Somehow
Although from a different place
It is always the same

High Street Folkestone, Kent
Narrow cobbled thoroughfare
Brightly painted shops
Lifting moods in a moment
Really got to smile
And we usually do

The Harbour Folkestone, Kent
Water glistens in the midday sun
Boats of all sizes shimmer in the heat
Walking the Harbour Arm

To see a little better

Feeling at peace

Beach huts Folkestone, Kent

Tiny homes from home

For the select few

Are they art?

We certainly would say so

Resplendent in pastel hues

We adore Folkestone, Kent

All life going on

A family plays catch-ball on the sand

Three generations laughing together

It's that kind of place

Happy times

Port of Sheppey

Cars

Cars stretch out towards the horizon

Thousands or tens of thousands perhaps

Destined for British roads

Viewing this vista with mixed feelings

I have enjoyed new cars myself in bygone days

That unique "newness" smell inside

I totally get the allure

And yet…

Looking at all this I cannot help but ponder

When did we become such a throwaway society?

Is it more eco-friendly to buy a new eco-friendly car?

With its massive manufacturing carbon footprint

And equally expansive importation carbon footprint

Asking the question

I wonder if we would be wiser to keep our cars as long as they serve us well

And is this in reality more eco-friendly?

Hmmm....

Tony

A tribute to Maidstone born artist and television presenter Tony Hart (1925-2009) and his absolute passion for inspiring children to create art for themselves.

The smaller version of me is watching Take Hart
I love Morph and his crazy antics
Most of all though I feel compelled to pick up a paintbrush
Tony makes it look so easy
I create a moonscape just as he had
Entered into a local art competition without my knowledge
This work of art inspired by my friend on television
And I won the under-ten's prize
When they gave me my certificate I thanked Tony Hart
Delight written large upon my face

This gentle gentleman was part of my childhood
Part of so many children's childhood
I owe being an artist and poet to this man
He showed me possibilities
Tony Hart I salute you
You were one of a kind

Promenading In Hythe

The surprisingly derided Hythe is actually rather wonderful, the uncommercial seafront makes for a peaceful walk with magical views...

I have found an open mind especially useful on my travels
Regardless of these travels being to places or through life
How often one and the same
As I anticipated a walk in Hythe for the first time
For sure I had read about it
I prefer to reach my own conclusions
We would walk the promenade for as far as felt we wanted
And then retrace our steps after a suitable picnic

First impressions
This town is gloriously uncommercialised
Oh there are hotels and guest houses
Yet none of the trappings of a typical seaside town
I like this

The promenade is quiet this early summer's morning
A few cyclists hurry past and a couple walk their dog

And that's about it at this time of the day
We seem to be past the rows of buildings lining the seafront in no time at all

Shingly beach to the right of us bringing the tide in towards us
Waves lap gently
The white Imperial Hotel stood facing the sea
As we saunter onwards towards Sandgate
A Martello tower and history made large at the castle
I might have mentioned I love Martello towers!
Seems like a good point to rest and eat
Our picnic serving as late breakfast

Suitably sustained we being to retrace our steps
It is busier now, not really busy, but busier
Upon reaching Hythe we stroll around the town
Once vital central Cinque Port
Now a relaxing place spend time window shopping
She asks me what I think of Hythe
"Rather wonderful and magical" can be my only reply

Gravesend Pier

I love seaside piers, I simply had to include a poem in homage to the iconic one in Gravesend in this collection.

The oldest cast iron pier in the world so they say
Cross the Thames by ferry, in Tilbury spend the day
The clock now works, it didn't when I was there
Stood leaning on the railing, taking in the sea air
Trying to imagine how it looked back in the mists of time
Like so many of its kind, it prospered then saw a decline
And yet here it stands proudly in the 21st century, relevant
Nearly two hundred years surviving open to the elements
Costing less than nine thousand pounds to build the deal
Gravesend pier that Clark designed and Wood made real

Not So Bleak House, Broadstairs

Although I am perhaps not the world's biggest fan of Dickens, looking as I did as a child rather identical to the boy who played the title role in the musical version of Oliver Twist and not particularly enjoying when well-meaning adults pointed out this fact to me for quite possibly the hundredth time! I nevertheless still resolved that I needed to spend a night staying at Bleak House. Just so that I could say I did and being a poet...

I had first been formerly introduced to Charles Dickens work when at high school
As David Copperfield we dissected over the course of a term
And we were told he wrote this book in Kent
Broadstairs to be precise, at the ominously named Bleak House
Upon a little research I discovered Charles had written a book of the same name
I decided one day I would see what all the fuss was about
I would visit Bleak House

Fast-forward a few decades and an opportunity presents itself
With room duly reserved, we arrive to book in for our short stay
And we are taken aback

This place looks and feels anything but bleak!

Could it have been so different back when Charles leased the house?

And then I remembered, of course he was a writer

Being a poet I put myself in his shoes for a little while and I got it.

He wrote social dramas, using people and places he knew for inspiration

As I also feel inclined to

And how often these people or places are layered with character and meaning to move along the story

Bleak House being not so bleak then not so much of a surprise

Returning To Rochester

This tells of a man who returns to his hometown of Rochester after many years, for he is a Morris Man and is there for the annual Sweeps Festival with his Morris side.

It started with an invitation to his Morris side
Come to fair Rochester
Take part in the Sweeps Festival
Celebrate Jack-In-The-Green
Ensure a good harvest for all

Like most places do given forty years away
Rochester had evolved. Changed a little
Taking a little time for him to get his bearings
The house he and his brothers were born in
now residing under shops

The Cathedral and Castle dominate the skyline

Twin points of familiarity

Reminding him of when the town was a city

Back when he walked these streets so long ago

Before he left to go to sea and never look back

The beginning of a life of true adventure

Taking him around the World

Too many stories to tell

Some other time perhaps…

Wandering his half familiar hometown

Overlooking the Medway, sitting on a bench

More trees, he observes

Or perhaps they were always there but unnoticed?

Smiling at the memories of his life here

Beginning to feel more alive

Finally venturing back to his fellow Morris Men

Enjoying dancing around Rochester

Seeking familiar faces in the crowds lining the streets.

Not finding any, yet still making happy new memories of his birthplace

Taking them with him back to the Oxfordshire town he now calls home

Dreams Of Kent

I am particularly pleased to get Kate Bush as a guest in one of my poems...

I like bridges and piers, in a parallel World I'm a civil engineer
in this World I am mostly civil and mostly sincere
I like architecture, in a parallel World I built Great Maytham Hall
in this World I just sketch buildings, taking in it all
I like trains, in a parallel World I drive them through to Calais
in this World no leaves or snow on the track is a good day
I like trees, in a parallel World I manage and care for Lyminge Forest
in this World against a tree I simply like to sit and rest
I like the coast, in a parallel World the whole of Kent I sail around
in this World I usually prefer both feet firmly on the ground
I like music, in a parallel World I play keyboards for Kate Bush
in this World poetry is my way of getting a rush

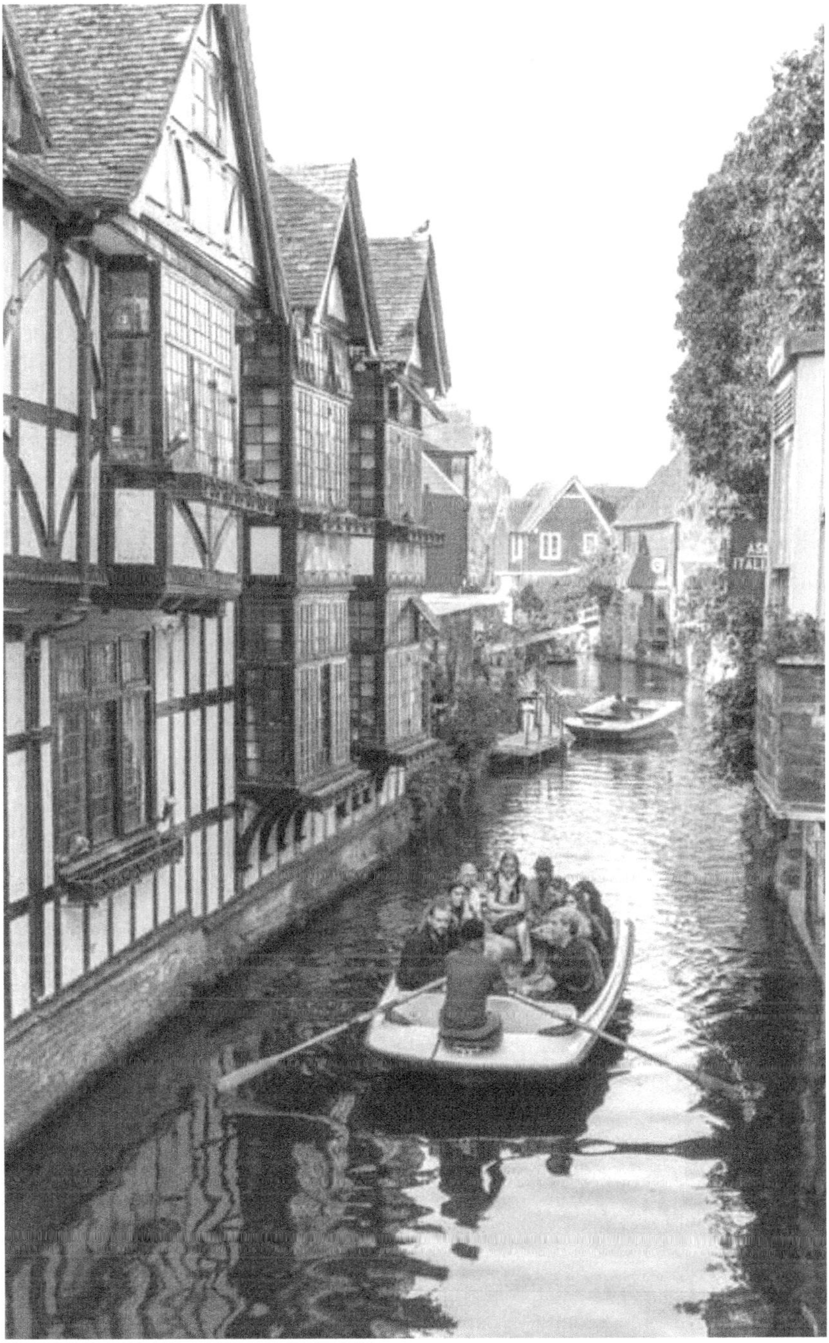

Trying To Avoid Thomas Becket

Not that I have anything in particular against him, rather that there seems so many more things to see in Canterbury that it became almost a personal challenge to not visit the shrine in his honour.

When I first heard of Thomas Becket as a small child
I wondered how the king could hate this man so much he had to die

By and by Canterbury became my nearest city
I duly walked the cloisters of the cathedral
Picnicked on the grassy bank within the grounds

I marvelled at the Crooked House on Palace Street
Walked in the footsteps of Romans around the walls
Visited The Beaney and spent many hours in the health food shop

I love Canterbury where the ancient sits alongside the modern
A riverboat tour taking in a new perspective of the city
Feeling a little of the Venetian experience

And yet for all that there are always new experiences
More places to explore it seems awaiting our attention
Except for the shrine, which can wait for another time.
Maybe…

There Was No Possibility Of Taking A Walk That Day

Whilst firstly begging the forgiveness of Charlotte Bronte for borrowing her famous opening line which proved such a good fit for the title of this poem, inspired by a visit to Botany Bay and Broadstairs with gales so strong we were actually unable to open the door of our car!

There is rain and then there is the torrential downpour which met us that winter's day
Having intended to take for ourselves the pleasure of a ramble around fair Botany Bay
Yet the weather had other ideas as we resigned ourselves to sitting and admiring the view
After all there will be other moments, other chances, even if this time our plan went askew

Happy Days At Bridge

We had acquired a new tent and wanted to test it first to see how easy it was erect before going on holiday, cue a walk in the fields around Bridge, near Canterbury.

Armed with instructions and our fresh from shop tent
For a little roam around the fields of Bridge we went
Finding the spot, just adjacent to the path of our choice
And up went our tent with ease, as we suitably rejoice

Sat inside testing out the space, it feels amazing to behold
Eventually taking it down once more, into its bag we fold
Easy to put up and spacious we agree are fantastic pros
The only downside to carry it feels like about fifty kilos!

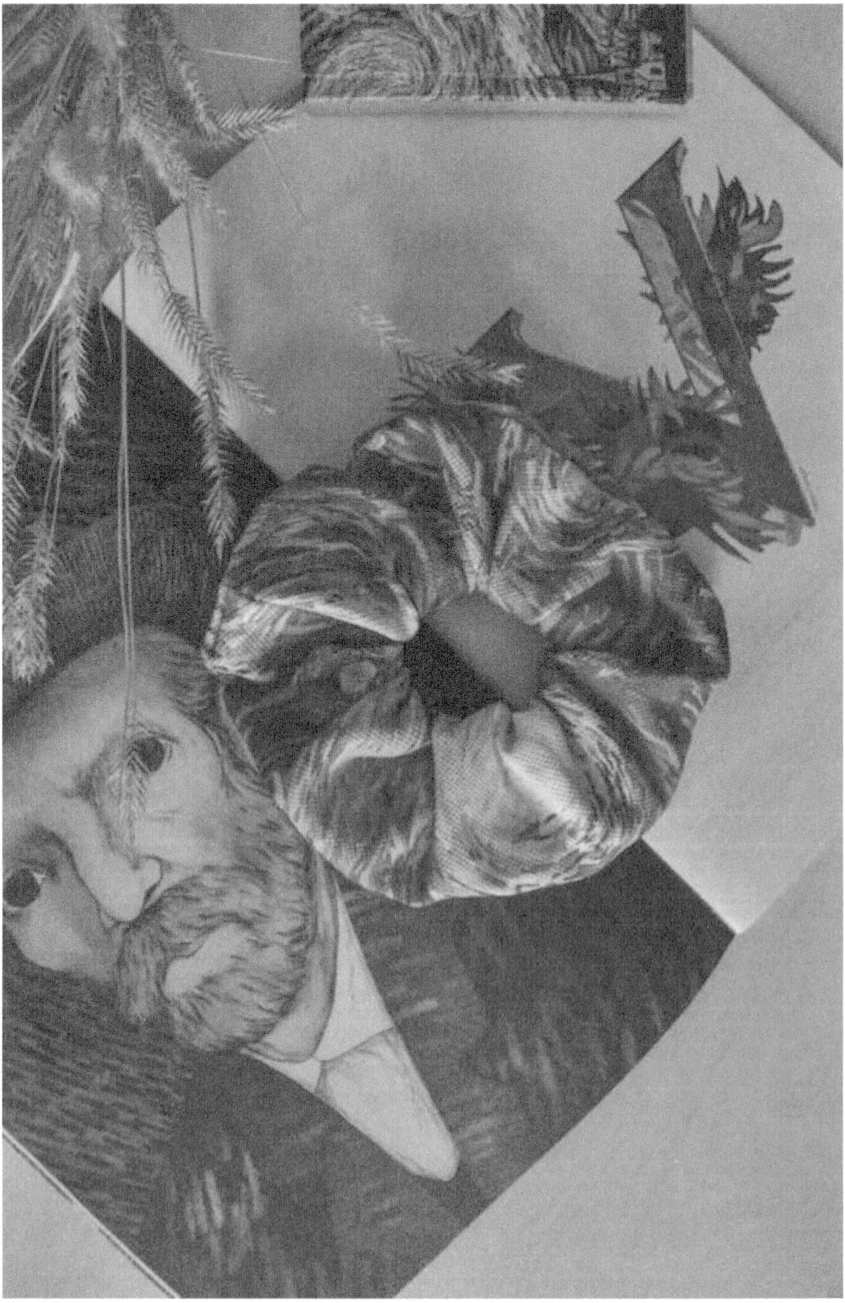

Finding Van Gogh In Ramsgate

Vincent hadn't been lost, rather this poem explores my surprise upon first discovering he had lived in the town for around a year.

The last time I had made his acquaintance was in New York
His Mountains at Saint-Rémy hangs resplendent in The Guggenheim
And I was entranced coming face to face with Vincent's art in frame
Vividly he depicted his visions of the world, so full of passion and energy

The memory stayed with me…

Finding a bust of Vincent in Ramsgate felt peculiarly odd
He lived in Spencer Square apparently, a blue plaque to confirm this
Working as a teacher at the local school when a young man himself
He liked Ramsgate; he wrote his brother that he loved the naturalness of the sea

Vincent my friend, I would have to agree…

Dartford On The Map

There really is nowhere else in Kent sharing quite the uniqueness of Dartford…

The industrial past
Paper making, brewing, cement
Dartford has seen it all and then some

Arts and culture
Visionary pop artist Peter Blake born here
The Mick Jagger Centre named after another famous son

The natural landscape
Not as famous as its namesake is Central Park
The industrial past turned transformed into a shopping centre

Civil engineering wonder
I remember long ago travelling through the tunnel
Now Dartford Crossing a functional yet beautiful gateway to Kent

Chatham Naval Memorial

Obelisk stood out against azure blue sky

In honour of fallen townsmen

Unimaginable horror of two world wars

Twenty thousand names

As near as

Listed for all to see

Lest we forget

A reminder of the fragility of human life

But not humanity

Tonbridge Times

The historical significance of the town provided ample inspiration here… and modern observations to finish the tale.

You'll find it in the Domesday Book
If you care to take a look
Was it named after one bridge or more?
We will perhaps never know for sure

A castle came and went then came once more
Council offices now, receded threat of war
England's first speeding ticket as justice served
With a heady speed of 8mph fine well deserved

The Oast Theatre stands loud and proud
Transformed function arts playing to a full crowd
Beautiful walks taking in the town on foot to see
Angel Gardens resplendent in the cause of bees

The Man Who Changed Everything

Poetry telling of a man born in Sheerness, namely Dr Beeching. This is the man who changed the railways and the landscape of this country forever; and yet Heritage Railways would never have happened if it were not for his cost cutting exercises and steam might well no longer be able to be enjoyed. Perhaps it is time re-assess the impact of Dr Beeching?

1960's the railways needed to profit, pay their way
Dr Beeching tasked to make it happen, the final say
Brutally, with logic his tool, he closed stations and lines
All part of his greater plan, about efficiency and time
Seven thousand miles of closures over twenty years
Cutting off communities, his quest brought many tears

By and by Heritage Lines began appearing on lines he axed

Happy people travelling as before, trains blowing stacks

Five choices alone in fair Kent to go live the dream

To venture back in time a little and do it by steam

It Must Be Faldo

The place is Sandwich during the British Open Golf, and a case of mistaken identity back in the early 1990's, as related to me many years later by a friend.

Faldo, he's my favourite golfer
I recognise him from TV
Look, it must be him

He's going into that supermarket
Let's follow to be sure
For certain, it must be him!

Be discrete, play it cool
Keep our distance
I am sure, it must be him!

Look he's at the till now
Talking to the checkout woman
Oh, it isn't him…

Faversham Market

A tale of visiting the market and the diversity of choice available to the casual shopper.

Its reputation preceded it
Faversham Charter Market the location in question
On a Saturday
Traders vie for attention
Fruit and veg, clothes and electrical goods
Seems anything can be bought
Enjoying the hustle and bustle
A time of commerce and growing

Yet here is also another market
On this summer's day
Arts, crafts and food it seems
Adding to our experience in the town
Buying olives and fresh falafels
Later relaxing bench in Recreation Ground
Sitting eating our purchases
One day we shall return once more… one day…

Talisman For Sittingbourne

The sculpture on the High Street gave me inspiration here.

Man in bronze frozen in time

Silently he observes Sittingbourne

Once barges were vital

Here he laboured

Come rain or shine

Stood at his wheel

Just as he was cast

To remind the people

She Was A Teacher

A poetic tribute to MCC and our time spent together. She proved to be the most enthusiastic guide to Kent I could have wished for.

She taught in the primary school
I jokingly always brought an apple along on our adventures
Should teacher ever want one
And did we ever explore!
Coast, countryside and off the beaten track
And all the while she shared her extensive knowledge of Kent
She loved to travel, often frequently far-flung places
Yet she made our more local travels compelling

I write this book in the memory of MCC.

She who passed far too soon

This collection could never have never happened without you

The Coldrum Stones

The story of an early morning visit to this ancient site in Medway.

The sun provided welcome warmth as it arose

We were there early that winter's day

Wanting that place to ourselves

Coldrum with eerily skeletal tree alongside

Offerings made by those there before us

Crystal and ribbons bedecked

Predating Stonehenge this site

Sat reaching far into the past

Communing with our ancient ancestors

Atmospheric mist drifted across the fields

Feeling at peace in that place

Feeling at one with everything

Visiting Folkestone In Winter

A visit in inclement weather provided the inspiration for this poetic tale.

Walking along the seafront doing my best to look dignified
Yet the gale force wind has other ideas
Icy cold rain finding its way through many layers of clothing
Wind hitting me squarely in the back
Propelling me forward
Trying not to run

Not so many people around today
Although a few hardy dog walkers pass me by
We say hello through wind made tears
Amazed anyone would choose to walk today
Perhaps their dogs insisted…

Continuing walking
No, running towards the centre of Folkestone
Nature providing unneeded assistance
I buy chips…
Seems like the thing to do in this weather

Holding hot food, warming frozen fingers

Sitting in the shelter… eating

Storm rages all around

I am philosophizing

As the feeling in my hands returns a little

This is a day I just feel happy to be alive!

The Longer Journey

You can visit mainland Europe easily from here

Gateway to everywhere it seems

And yet Kent looks lovely whatever the season

The Garden Of England for sure

And in all honestly why go anywhere else?

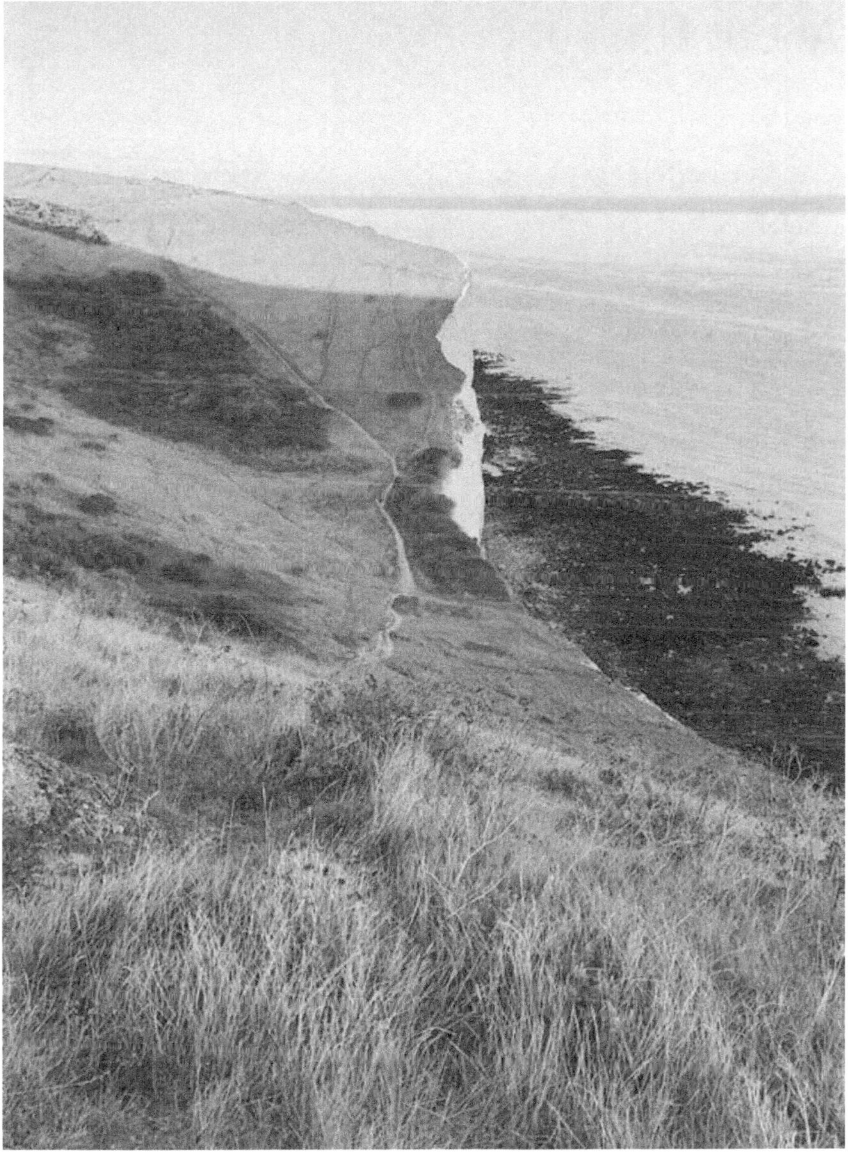

About The Poet

Over the last three plus decades I have worked as an artist; owned a wholesale business selling crystal healing kits, dowsing pendulums and books; spent time as an antique dealer and ran an events company. I qualified in Body Language Psychology twenty-five years ago. All the while during this time I have also brought positive energy into other's lives through sharing my travel poetry.

Brightest Blessings Dean Fraser

Poetry Books And Audios

By Dean Fraser

A Healing For Gaia

Beyond Poetry

The Kent Poems

The Poems Less Spoken

Travels With My Notebook & Pen

Available from Amazon and all good bookstores.

Travels With My Notebook & Pen

Let's WANDER Where the Wi-Fi is weak

Dean Fraser

The Poems Less Spoken

Rarities and Previously Unreleased Poetry

Dean Fraser

I hope that you enjoyed this poetic journey with me… love and peace good people… love and peace.

To hire Dean Fraser to perform from The Kent Poems at your event visit www.alivetothrive.co.uk request a quote